NMAP 7

Simple Guide on Network Scanning

William Rowley

**Copyright©2017 William Rowley
All Rights Reserved**

Copyright © 2017 by William Powley

All rights reserved. No part of this publication may be reproduced, distributed, or transmitted in any form or by any means, including photocopying, recording, or other electronic or mechanical methods, without the prior written permission of the author, except in the case of brief quotations embodied in critical reviews and certain other noncommercial uses permitted by copyright law.

Table of Contents

Introduction	5
Chapter 1- Getting Started with Nmap	6
Chapter 2- Scanning for SMB Vulnerabilities	12
Chapter 3- Scanning for Open Ports	14
Chapter 4- Testing for HeartBleed Bug	18
Chapter 5- Detecting Live Hosts	21
Chapter 6- Firewall Scanning	24
Chapter 7- Performing Layer 2 Discovery	34
Chapter 8- Banner Grabbing	37
Chapter 9- Information Gathering	39
Chapter 10- Penetrating into Servers	41
Conclusion	44

Disclaimer

While all attempts have been made to verify the information provided in this book, the author does assume any responsibility for errors, omissions, or contrary interpretations of the subject matter contained within. The information provided in this book is for educational and entertainment purposes only. The reader is responsible for his or her own actions and the author does not accept any responsibilities for any liabilities or damages, real or perceived, resulting from the use of this information.

The trademarks that are used are without any consent, and the publication of the trademark is without permission or backing by the trademark owner. All trademarks and brands within this book are for clarifying purposes only and are the owned by the owners themselves, not affiliated with this document.

Introduction

With the advancement in technology, Internet users have been exposed to much information on how to hack into computer networks. There are also numerous programs on the Internet which can be downloaded for free and used to hack into the computer networks. This calls for organizations to stay alert and staying sure that their network system is secure. Nmap is a tool which can help you carry out a penetration test on your network so to determine some of its loopholes. Such loopholes can be sealed early enough before an attack by a malicious user can occur. This can help in safeguarding the sensitive data for the organization. This book guides you on how to perform a network penetration test on your network so as to stay safe. Enjoy reading!

Chapter 1- Getting Started with Nmap

Nmap is simply a network scanner. It helps in tasks such as firewall detection, port scanning, network scanning, IP scanning, and others. The tool is available for free, and one can use it for scanning ports, website status, live hosts, and for pinging. This tool is good for hackers, as it helps them locate hosts and services so as to create a map from that.

Nmap 7 comes with several scripts which can help you do nearly everything including Doing the targets to exploit them. Such scripts include the following:

- **Auth:** used to test whether one can bypass the authentication mechanism.

- **Broadcast:** used to find the other hosts on a network and add them automatically to the scanning queue.

- **Brute:** used for brute password guessing.

- **Discovery:** used for discovering more about the network.

- **Dos:** used for testing whether the target is vulnerable to Denial of Service (DoS) attacks.

- **Exploit:** used for actively exploiting vulnerability.

- **Fuzzer:** used for testing how the server responds to the unexpected or randomized fields in the packets, and then determining the other potential vulnerabilities

- **Intrusive:** used to do more intense scans which pose a higher risk of detection by the admins.

- **Malware:** used to test the target for the presence of malware.

- **Safe:** used to perform a general network security scan which is less likely to alarm the remote administrators.

- **Vuln:** used to find the vulnerabilities on the target.

Setting up Nmap

Nmap is available on the **https://nmap.org/download.html** directory. One should download the right version based on the operating system they are using. The installation steps for Nmap are also different for the different operating systems. In the case of Windows, you have to download the .exe file with the nmap tool, and then double click it so as to begin executing it. You will first be asked to agree to the licensing terms:

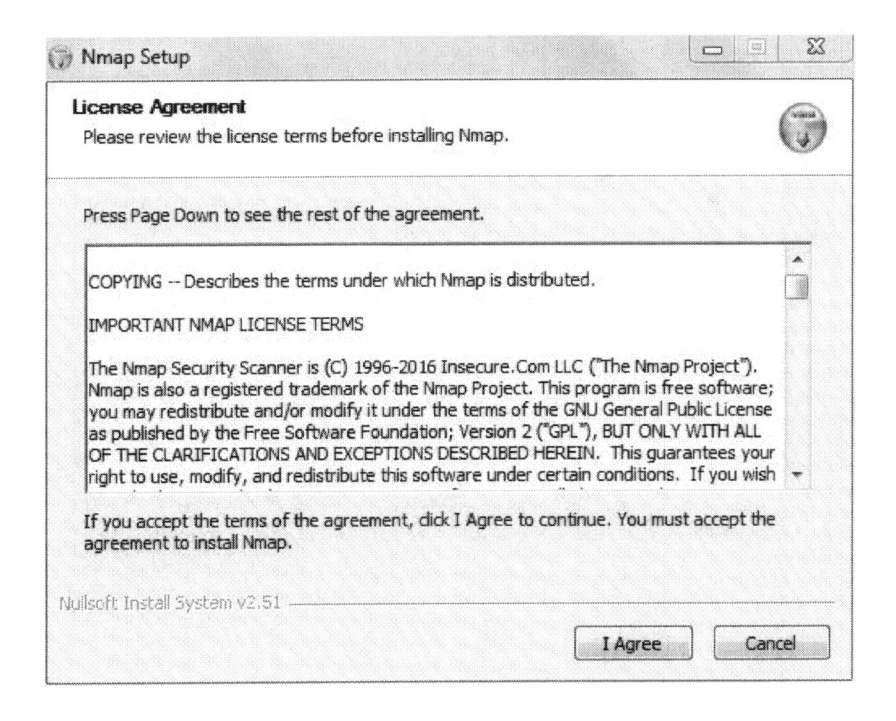

![Nmap Setup License Agreement dialog]

Next, you will be asked to choose the features which should be installed. It is good for you to leave it at the default setting, and then you click on Next:

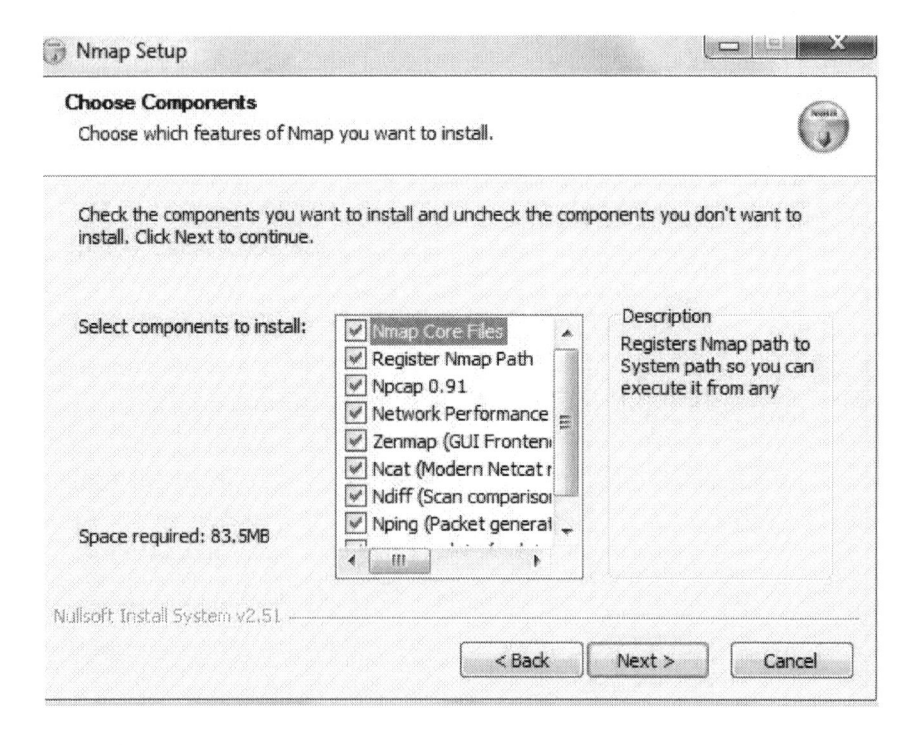

In the next window, choose the directory in which you want to install the nmap, and then click on Install. The installation process will begin right away.

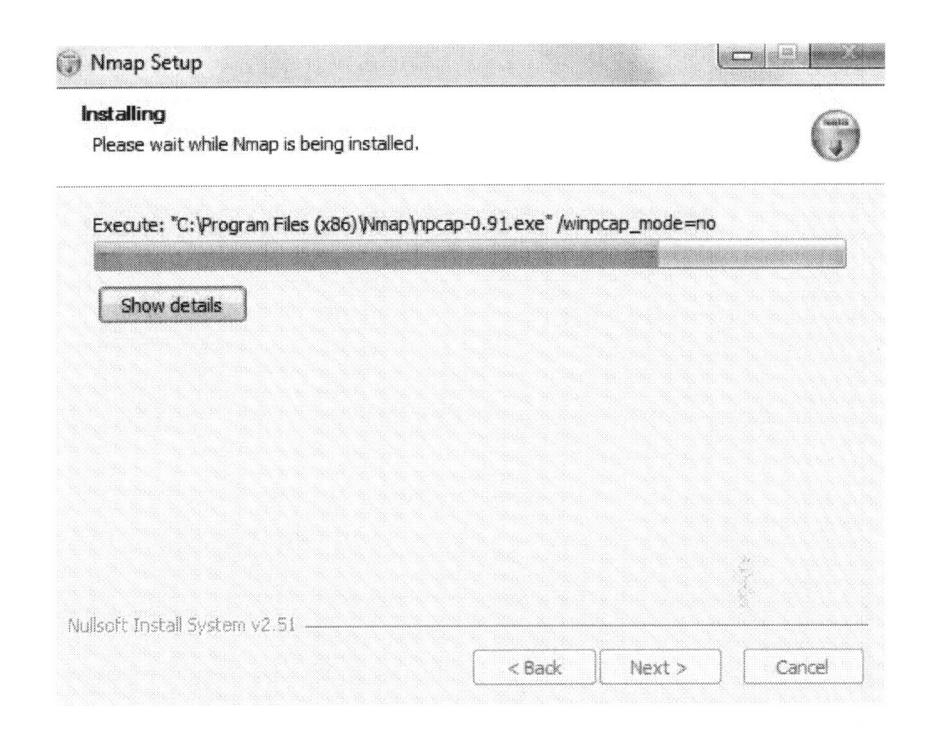

![Nmap Setup - Installing screen showing "Execute: C:\Program Files (x86)\Nmap\npcap-0.91.exe /winpcap_mode=no" with a progress bar and Show details button]

Note that the nmap for Windows is not as efficient as the nmap for Linux. Let us demonstrate how nmap can be installed and updated on the earlier versions of Kali Linux.

Before performing the update, first ensure that you have all the repositories in place. The following command can help you verify this:

cat /etc/apt/sources.list

The official repositories for Kali Linux 2.0 include the following:

deb http://http.kali.org/kali sana main non-free contrib

deb http://security.kali.org/kali-security sana/updates main contrib non-free

deb-src http://http.kali.org/kali sana main non-free contrib

deb-src http://security.kali.org/kali-security sana/updates main contrib non-free

The repositories for the older versions include the following:

deb http://http.kali.org/kali kali main non-free contrib

deb http://security.kali.org/kali-security kali/updates main contrib non-free

deb-src http://http.kali.org/kali kali main non-free contrib

deb-src http://security.kali.org/kali-security kali/updates main contrib non-free

If you don't have the above, then you can copy them and add them to the file "sources.list" which can be found in the "/etc/apt/" directory. You can then update the package database for the OS by running the following command:

apt-get update

The update will take some minutes, which will be determined by the number of updates to be done and the speed of your Internet connection. Once the update is completed, you will be ready to install a newer version.
You only have to install nmap again. Using apt-get will update the version you have to the latest version:

apt-get install nmap

After the installation completes, verify the version that you have by using the –V option as shown below:

nmap –V

Now that you have updated the nmap package, you can go ahead and update the zenmap package. To do this, launch the terminal, and then run the following command:

apt-get install zenmap

Chapter 2- Scanning for SMB Vulnerabilities

Nmap 7 comes with numerous scripts. In this chapter, we will be using a script to scan a target host for SMB vulnerabilities. SMB is an acronym for Server Message Blocks. The SMB1 is commonly used in Windows XP and Windows 2000. These two were capable of allowing null sessions which can be used to give information about a target machine. The later versions of the SMB are also prone to a number of vulnerabilities which can allow the stealing of remote user credentials and the remote execution of code. This explains why one should check SMB during any penetration test.

We will make use of the NMap scripts so as to scan our target host for SMB vulnerabilities. Nmap comes with the Nmap Scripting Engine (NSE) which is a very powerful and flexible feature. This scripting engine has also been expanded in Nmap 7. The following command can help you to execute the Nmap with a script:

nmap --script [scriptname]-p [port][host]

In case the command gives an error, add the --script-args=unsafe=1 to it so that you can get the status for the SMB vulnerabilities. This is shown below:

nmap --script [scriptname]--script-args=unsafe=1 -p [port][host]

If you need the Nmap to scan a particular host for vulnerabilities, use the command given below:

nmap --script smb-check-vulns.nse --script-args=unsafe=1 -p445 [host]

The following command will show you all the SMB shares on your target host:

nmap --script smb-enum-shares.nse --script-args=unsafe=1 -p445 [host]

Nmap also provides you with a script for OS discovery, and this makes use of SMB as shown below:

nmap --script smb-os-discovery.nse --script-args=unsafe=1 -p445 [host]

You can see the users of your target host by running the following command:

nmap --script smb-enum-users.nse --script-args=unsafe=1 -p445 [host]

One can also use Nmap to scan their host for the MS17-010 Eternalblue. This can be applied to a single target host or a range of hosts. Before we can do this, we should first download the smb-vuln-ms12-010.nse script which can be obtained from the link given below:

https://raw.githubusercontent.com/cldrn/nmap-nse-scripts/master/scripts/smb-vuln-ms17-010.nse

The file should be stored in the Nmap directory for scripts. The following command will then help you to launch the attacks:

nmap -p 445 -script=smb-vuln-ms17-010.nse [host]

The following command will help you to target the hosts in the local network:

nmap -p 445 -script=smb-vuln-ms17-010.nse [host-range]

Chapter 3- Scanning for Open Ports

In this chapter, we will use OS Detection to scan for the open ports on a system. We will begin with a Linux system. Remember that Zenmap provides you with a graphical user interface (GUI) for using Nmap.

We will first use an IP range so as to do a ping scan and determine the live hosts. The following command will help us accomplish this:

nmap -sP 192.168.0.0-100

We can use one of the live hosts and perform a SYN scan with OS Detection on it. This is shown below:

nmap -sS [ip address]-O

We can now do a port scan with version detection by running the following command:

nmap -sV 192.168.0.1 –A

To make the command more verbose on the command line, we can use the –v option as shown below:

nmap -sV 192.168.0.13 -A –v

That is it!

If you need to see all the ports which are available on your system, just run the following command:

less /etc/services

This will show you some of the common ports, together with the services associated with them.

It is always good for you to use the server provided at scanme.nmap.org for testing purposes. You can use the sudo command so that you can the full results after executing commands. If you need to scan the host operating system, you can run the following command:

sudo nmap -O remote_host

Sometimes, you may get a response saying "Note: Host seems down." In such a case, you can skip the option for network discovery, and then assume that your host is online. The following should be added to the other hosts:

sudo nmap -PN remote_host

If you need to scan a number of hosts at once, then you can us a "-" or a "/". This is demonstrated below:

sudo nmap -PN xxx.xxx.xxx.xxx-yyy

If you need to determine the available services for a network range, then you can use the command given below:

sudo nmap -sP network_address_range

You can also perform the scan without having to perform a reverse DNS lookup on the specified IP address. In most cases, this should speed up the results:

sudo nmap -n remote_host

If you are targeting a specific port rather than a range of ports, you can use the command shown below:

sudo nmap -p port_number remote_host

If you need to scan for the TCP connections, the nmap will perform a 3-way handshake with the target port. Just run the following:

sudo nmap -sT remote_host

The UDP connections can be scanned as shown below:

sudo nmap -sU remote_host

The following command will help you scan every UDP and TCP port which is open:

sudo nmap -n -PN -sT -sU -p- remote_host

A TCP "SYN" scan will reveal how TCP establishes a connection.

For the TCP connection to be established, the requesting end first sends a "synchronize request" packet to server. The server in turn will send a "synchronize acknowledgement" back to the sender. The sender will then send an "acknowledgement" packet to the server and the connection will be established.

In the case of the SYN scan, the connection is dropped once the server returns its first packet. This is usually referred to as a "half-open" scan. However, with the new advanced firewalls, this is no longer stealthy. A SYN scan is performed by running the following command:

sudo nmap -sS remote_host

One of the best approaches is the sending of invalid TCP headers, and if the host meets the TCP specifications, the packet will be sent back in case the port is closed. This will work on servers which are not based on Windows.

One may choose to use "-sF," "-sX," or "-sN" flags. These will help us get the response which we are looking for:

sudo nmap -PN -p port_number -sN remote_host

The following command will help you learn the version of the service which is running:

It will test different responses from the server so as to determine the services and their versions:

sudo nmap -PN -p port_number -sV remote_host

There exists as well a number of other combinations of commands.

Chapter 4- Testing for HeartBleed Bug

The heartbleed bug helps attackers to steal information which has been encrypted with the SSL/TLS encryption. This type of encryption is widely used for securing Internet connections. It is a very serious vulnerability in the OpenSSL cryptographic software library.

A fix for this bug has been invented and implemented in many operating systems, but when one uses a vulnerable version of the OpenSSL, this bug can still be exploited. This is also possible with applications which have not been patched by the vendor or the user.

With the SSL-Heartbleed script for Nmap, it will take us a short time to look for the vulnerability. Most web applications, software applications, and web services come with an integration of SSL/TLS encryption, and these can easily be affected by the heartbleed bug.

In this chapter, we will be using a WordPress server and Kali Linux which will be running in two separate VMware virtual machines. First, configure WordPress, and then fire up the Kali Linux VM. The Nmap script helps one detect the servers which are dso. You may have to install it manually.

Detecting the Exploit

You should first install the script if it is not available in your Nmap install. You just have to visit the **OpenSSL-Heartbleed nmap Script page** web page, copy the script, and save it in the scripts directory of Nmap in your computer. You should have the **nmap "tls.lua" library file**, and this should be saved in the "nselib" directory of nmap.

After that, you will be in a position to use the nmap script so as to detect the vulnerable systems. The command for this takes the following syntax:

nmap -sV --script=ssl-heartbleed <target>

We should only add in the IP address of the WordPress site we are targeting. In my case, I will end up with the following:

nmap -sV --script=ssl-heartbleed 192.168.160.1

In case the machine is vulnerable to this type of attack, you will see a section of the output with the following:

State:VULNERABLE
Risk Factor: High

This shows that it is vulnerable, and we can exploit this.

With the Metasploit OpenSSL-Heartbleed module, we can exploit the vulnerability we have detected on the server. We will use the latest version of this module. You should begin by updating Metasploit. Since you are using Kali Linux, launch its terminal, and then execute the "msfupdate" command and the update will be done.

Once the update is completed, launch the Metasploit console by running the "msfconsole" on the Kali Linux terminal. The Metasploit console will then be presented to you.

The next step should involve searching for the Heartbleed modules. On the Metasploit console, just run the "search heartbleed" command and this will be presented to you. The modules are two, but we only need to use the "scanner" module. Next, run the following command on the Metasploit console:

use auxiliary/scanner/ssl/openssl_heartbleed

You will see the prompt change.

```
msf auxiliary(openssl_heartbleed) >
```

To see the available options, just run the command "show options." We need to make the command verbose, so we will enable this feature. The "set VERBOSE" option should be set to true, while the "set RHOSTS" option should be set to the IP address which we are targeting.

To enable the verbose feature, run the following command:

set verbose true

The Rhosts feature can then be set to the target IP address by running the following command:

set rhosts 192.168.160.1

Lastly, you can execute the "run" command on the same console so as to run the exploit.

From the output that you get, you will notice that Metasploit was able to pull data from the server. Note that the data was pulled randomly from the server's memory. It is not a guarantee that you will get the credentials of the account, the cookies, or any other critical data. However, it is possible for this to display the server's sensitive data.

This shows the importance of checking systems for the Heartbleed vulnerability and if found, you seal it immediately. Once the systems have been patched, you can change the passwords of affected machines.

Chapter 5- Detecting Live Hosts

Detection of live hosts is one of the best tools in ethical hacking and penetration testing. In this chapter, we will be using Nmap on Kali Linux so as to scan the network for the live hosts.

The ifconfig command can be used if you want to determine the IP address range that you want to scan for the live hosts. A ping scan will be used on the range of the possible live hosts on the network. The nmap will then ping each host in the specified range so as to know whether the host is alive or not.

The nmap will be responsible for scanning and detecting the hosts which are available on the network.

The ping command will help us learn the connectivity of our network hosts. It will send an ICMP packet with 8 and 0 codes which indicates that the packet is an echo request. If the target receives this packet, it will reply with a 0, which indicates that this is a reply packet. If the ping runs successfully, then it will be an indication that the host is live.

Consider the nmap command given below:

nmap -sP 192.168.0.0-100

This command will return the list of the live hosts which are detected on the network. You may need to make the command more verbose. In such a case, you can add the –v option to the command. This is shown below:

nmap -sP 192.168.0.0-100 –v

The command will give you all the hosts which have been scanned, plus their corresponding status. Consider the following nmap command:

nmap -sn 192.168.56.0/24

In the above example, we are using a 192.168.56.x, which is a class C address range. This means that the scan can only incorporate a maximum number of 254 hosts. The following command can help us to get a large number of scanned hosts:

nmap -sn 192.168.56.100-150

We may also choose to use CIDR (classless inter-domain routing) so as to solve the same problem. Since it is a class C address, we will use the /24 postfix.

We can also choose to use nmap with a list scan. In this case, a record with the Ip addresses to be scanned should be created and given a name. Suppose that we add the addresses in the file List.txt. The scanning can be performed by executing the following command:

#nmap –iL /Location_List.txt

This will show you the live hosts on the network. When you are scanning a large network of hosts, it is possible for you to exclude some of the hosts. Such hosts will not be scanned. This can be done by adding the –exclude option and specifying the IP addresses of the hosts to be excluded. The following command best demonstrates this:

nmap 192.168.1.0/24 --exclude 192.168.1.5
nmap 192.168.1.0/24 --exclude 192.168.1.5,192.168.1.254

Note that in the first command, we are excluding only a single host. In the second command, we are excluding two hosts, and their IP addresses have been separated by use of a comma. If you have more hosts which should be excluded in the scan, then separate their IP addresses by use of a comma.

If the hosts to be scanned are contained in a list, you can still exclude some. This is demonstrated by the command given below:

nmap -iL /tmp/scanlist.txt --excludefile /tmp/exclude.txt

Chapter 6- Firewall Scanning

With firewalls, mapping a network can be difficult. It is always good for you to test your firewall rules and know whether they are working as expected. This will give you an impression of how your network looks to the external world and whether it is providing the expected level of security or not.

In this chapter, we will use nmap to test this, and we will combine it with tcpdumb. The latter is a packet analyzer tool which can help us to monitor all the traffic on a particular port. With some packet analyzers, you can analyze your traffic in real time. The tcpdumb tool will help us capture raw traffic.

We will then use the port scanner tool so as to generate the traffic which is to be analyzed by our packet analyzer. The port scanner tool can be used for generating the various types of traffic to the remote hosts so as to know the types of traffic which the server is capable of accepting. Nmap will be used as the port scanning tool. It will help us send different types of traffic so as to know the services which are on the target machine. The firewall rules which protect this will also be known.

Preparing the Auditing Machine

Before beginning to set up the auditing machine, ensure that you have the tools discussed above, the nmap and tcpdump tools. The tcpdump tool can be obtained from the Ubuntu repositories. The nmap tool can also be obtained from same repository, but it may be out of date. We will install a software package which will help us in the compilation and build it from the source.

Begin by updating the local package index, and then install the software if you had not installed it beforw. The nmap will also be purged from the system if it had not been installed so as to avoid any conflicts. Just run the commands given below:

sudo apt-get update
sudo apt-get purge nmap
sudo apt-get install tcpdump build-essential libssl-dev

My assumption is that you have the nmap tool already installed. If you don't have it, visit its official website and download it from there. You don't have to download it directly, but just copy its URL. Change to your home directory and use the wget command so as to download it as shown below:

cd ~
wget https://nmap.org/dist/nmap-6.49BETA4.tar.bz2

Once the download is complete, decompress the file which you have just downloaded and change to that directory:

tar xjvf nmap*
cd nmap*

After a complete compilation, install the executables which you get as well as the supporting files by running the following command:

sudo make install

You can confirm whether the installation was successful by checking the available nmap version with the following command:

nmap –V

We can then create a new directory which will be used for storing the scan results. This can be created as follows:

mkdir ~/scan_results

For clean results, exit the sessions which are open between the target system and the auditing system. These include the HTTP(s) and SSH connections which you might have established.

At this point, the server and the files are ready, so we can scan the target host and determine any open TCP ports. A SYN scan will be the best since it will not negotiate for a full TCP connection.

Preparing to capture the Packets

We should now setup the tcpdump so that it can capture the packets which are generated by nmap. This will give us a chance to analyze the pattern of traffic flow. We can now create a directory whose name is related to that of "scan-results," and this will be used for storing the files which are related to the SYN scan:

mkdir ~/scan_results/syn_scan

We can then start a capture with the tcpdump tool and store its results in the ~/scan_results/syn_scan directory. The following command will help us achieve this:

sudo tcpdump host target_ip_addr -w ~/scan_results/syn_scan/packets

The default setting is that the tcpdump will run in the foreground. For us to run nmap on the same window, we will have to pause the tcpdump, and then start it in the background.

Press CTRL-Z so as to pause the tcpdump:

CTRL-Z

The process will be paused, and then start in the background by running the bg command:

Bg

Now that the tcpdump command is running on the system, we are ready to run nmap. There are a number of flags that we will use so as to ensure that nmap does the work we want it to do. The complete nmap command should be as follows:

sudo nmap -sS -Pn -p- -T4 -vv --reason -oN ~/scan_results/syn_scan/nmap.results target_ip_addr

Even after setting the timing template to 4, the scanning process will take some time since a total of 65,535 ports will be scanned. As the scanning process continues, you will see results printed on the terminal.

After the scanning process completes, the tcdump process can be brought back to the foreground. We can then stop it. To bring it to the foreground, run the "fg" command as follows:

Fg

You can then stop the process by pressing CTRL-C:

CTRL-C

The process will be stopped.

Result Analysis

Your ~/scan_results/syn_scan directory should now have two files. One will be called packets, which will have been generated by the tcpdump, and the nmap.results which will have been generated by nmap.

You can first look at the nmap.results file by running the following command:

less ~/scan_results/syn_scan/nmap.results

You will be able to see that some ports will be open, the closed ports and the ones which are filtered. If you need to have a view of the packet traffic which was received from a target, the packets file can be read into the tcpdump by running the command given below:

sudo tcpdump -nn -r ~/scan_results/syn_scan/packets | less

This file will have all the conversation done between the two hosts. There are a number of ways that you can filter this. If you need to view only the traffic which was sent to the target, run the following command:

sudo tcpdump -nn -r ~/scan_results/syn_scan/packets 'dst target_ip_addr' | less

If you need to see only the response traffic, you only have to change the "dst" to "src" as shown below:

sudo tcpdump -nn -r ~/scan_results/syn_scan/packets 'src target_ip_addr' | less

The open TCP ports should respond to the requests with a SYN packet. It is possible for us to use a filter so as to search for such responses. This is shown below:

sudo tcpdump -nn -r ~/scan_results/syn_scan/packets 'src target_ip_addr and tcp[tcpflags] & tcp-syn != 0' | less

The command will give you all the SYN responses which are successful, and the ports seen in the nmap run should be seen.

Scanning for Open UDP Ports

At this point, we can scan to determine the UDP ports which are open. We should begin by creating a directory where we will store our results. This can be created as follows:

mkdir ~/scan_results/udp_scan

Launch a tcpdump capture. The file should be written to the ~/scan_results/udp_scan directory, which we have created above. This can be started as follows:

sudo tcpdump host target_ip_addr -w ~/scan_results/udp_scan/packets

You can press CTRL-Z to pause the process, and then send it to the background by running the "bg" command.

Running a UDP Scan

You may not have time for this test, but you may need to test only a section of the UDP ports. You may choose to test only the 1,000 ports which are common by leaving the –p- flag. This will make the scan time shorter. However, if you need a complete scan, then you will have to scan the entire port range.

If you need to speed up the scanning process, you have to disable the ICMP rate limiting temporarily on the target system. To see this rate on your machine, you can run the following command:

sudo sysctl net.ipv4.icmp_ratelimit

To disable this feature on the target system, just run the following command:

sudo sysctl -w net.ipv4.icmp_ratelimit=0

The Test

You should ensure that you write the results to the ~/scan_results/udp_scan directory. The command for testing should be as follows:

sudo nmap -sU -Pn -p- -T4 -vv --reason -oN ~/scan_results/udp_scan/nmap.results target_ip_addr

Even though you have disabled the ICMP rate limiting feature, the scan might still take a longer time. Once the scan completes, the ICMP rate limiting on the target machine should be reverted by running the following command:

sudo sysctl -w net.ipv4.icmp_ratelimit=1000

It is now time for you to stop the packet capture process by the tcpdump tool. Bring this process to the foreground on the audit machine by running the following command:

Fg

Hit Ctrl-C so as to end the packet capture process.

Results Analysis

It is now time for us to have a look at the files which have been generated. This should be the nmap.results file and it can be viewed by running the following command:

less ~/scan_results/udp_scan/nmap.results

For the SYN and UDP scans, you will notice that there is difference between ports marked open|filtered. This is an indication that nmap was unable to tell whether the lack of response means that the traffic was accepted by the service or whether some firewall dropped it, or there was some filtering mechanism along the path.

It is also hard for us to analyze the UDP traffic since there are no connection flags and that the ICMP responses must be matched to the UDP requests.

It is clear that nmap had to send so many requests to ports which had been marked as open|filtered by asking to view the UDP traffic to any of the ports.

**sudo tcpdump -nn -Q out -r
~/scan_results/udp_scan/packets 'udp and port 22'**

You can compare this to results obtained from one of the scanned ports which had been marked as "closed."

**sudo tcpdump -nn -Q out -r
~/scan_results/udp_scan/packets 'udp and port 53'**

We can then reconstruct the process which nmap has to go through by creating a list of all ports which were sending UDP packets. This is shown below:

**sudo tcpdump -nn -Q out -r
~/scan_results/udp_scan/packets "udp" | awk '{print $5;}'
| awk 'BEGIN { FS = "." } ; { print $5 +0}' | sort -u | tee
outgoing**

You will see the ICMP packets which were received back terming the port as unreachable:

**sudo tcpdump -nn -Q in -r
~/scan_results/udp_scan/packets "icmp" | awk '{print
$10,$11}' | grep unreachable | awk '{print $1}' | sort -u | tee
response**

We can use the two responses to see the UDP packets which did not receive an ICMP response. The following command will help us see this:

comm -3 outgoing response

This has to match the list of the ports which were reported by nmap.

Determining the Service Versions

We can use a process known as fingerprinting so as to determine the versions of services which are running on the server.

The information will be retrieved from the server, and this will be compared to the versions which we have kept in our database. Atcpdump will not be useful to us, but if you need to use it, just follow the usual steps discussed previously.

We want to use an nmap scan which will be triggered by the use of the –sV flag. Since we have done the SYN and the UDP scans, we are able to specify the exact ports which we need to explore by passing the –p option. Let us have a look at the ports which were shown in the SYN scan, the ports 22 and 80.

sudo nmap -sV -Pn -p 22,80 -vv --reason -oN ~/scan_results/versions/service_versions.nmap target_ip_addr

After viewing the resultant file, you will see the information regarding the service as it runs. This will be determined by how unique our service response is:

less ~/scan_results/versions/service_versions.nmap

In my case, the test identified the version of SSH server, the Linux distro which packaged it and the version of SSH protocol which accepted it. The version of Nginx was also identified, and that it matches the Ubuntu package.

Discovering the Operating System

The nmap tool can also help us detect the type of operating system being used based on the response as well as the software which is being used there. This works in the same manner as service versioning. The tcpdump will not be used, but in case you want to, just use it.

The detection of the operating system is done by use of the –O option. Note that the letter O is written in uppercase. The following command demonstrates this:

**sudo nmap -O -Pn -vv --reason -oN
~/scan_results/versions/os_version.nmap target_ip_addr**

You can then run the following command so as to view the contents of the output file:

less ~/scan_results/versions/os_version.nmap

You will observe that nmap will not have the guesses for the operating system. This is because it has not received much information which can help it make the guesses. The fingerprint signature which nmap received from the target will also be visible.

If it is possible for one to perform operating system detection, then this is useful to an attacker, as they may know the type of exploits which can be done on the system. That is why it is good for you to configure the firewall so that it can only respond to fewer requests or even give less accurate information. This way, your network will remain secure.

Chapter 7- Performing Layer 2 Discovery

The Nmap tool can be used to perform a layer 2 scan. For you to use the nmap tool for ARP discovery, your LAN should have at least one system which will be responding to your ARP requests. In this chapter, we will be using a combination of Linux and Windows systems.

With nmap, the layer 2 scans can be automated. This calls for us to use the –sn flag, which stands for a ping scan. If you specify the IP addresses which belongs to a similar subnet, the following command will help you perform a layer 2 scan:

nmap 172.16.36.133 –sn

The above command will send an ARP request to the AN broadcast address and the response received will help in determining whether the host is alive or not:

root@KaliLinux:~# nmap 172.16.36.133 –sn

Starting Nmap 6.25 (http://nmap.org) at 2017-7-27 15:40 EST

Nmap scan report for 172.16.36.133
Host is up (0.00038s latency).
MAC Address: 00:0C:27:3D:84:11 (VMware)

Nmap done: 1 IP address (1 host up) scanned in 0.17 seconds

Also, in case the IP address used is for a host which is not alive, then the response will tell you that the host is down. This is demonstrated below:

root@KaliLinux:~# nmap 172.16.36.136 -sn

Starting Nmap 6.25 (http://nmap.org) at 2017-7-27 15:51 EST

Note: Host seems down. If it is really up, but blocking our ping probes, try –Pn

Nmap done: 1 IP address (0 hosts up) scanned in 0.41 seconds

The command can also be modified so that it can perform a layer 2 discovery on a series of IP addresses by use of a dash notation. If you need to scan a full /24, then you should use 0-255. The following command demonstrates this:

nmap 172.16.36.0-255 –sn

The above command will help you to send out broadcast ARP requests for all the hosts which fall in the specified range, and it will identify all the hosts which are actively responding. We can also add the IP addresses to a list, and then use the –iL option so as to perform a scan on them. The following command demonstrates how this can be done:

nmap -iL iplist.txt –sn

With the use of the –sn option, the nmap tool will try to find the host by use of the ARP requests, and this will be done by use of only the layer 3 ICMP requests in case the host is not on the LAN. That is how an nmap ping scan can be done on the hosts which are located on the local network with the return being MAC addresses. The reason is that MAC addresses are returned by ARP response from hosts. However, in case you perform a similar nmap ping scan against the remote hosts which are on a different LAN, then the system MAC addresses will not be part of the response. The following example demonstrates this:

root@KaliLinux:~# nmap -sn 74.125.21.0-255

Starting Nmap 6.25 (http://nmap.org) at 2017-7-271 05:42 EST

Nmap scan report for 74.125.21.0
Host is up (0.0024s latency).
Nmap scan report for 74.125.21.1
Host is up (0.00017s latency).
Nmap scan report for 74.125.21.2
Host is up (0.00028s latency).
Nmap scan report for 74.125.21.3
Host is up (0.00017s latency).

When it has done a remote network range, you will observe that layer 3 discoveries was used, since no MAC addresses were returned. This is an indication that if it is possible, the nmap tool will leverage the layer 2 discovery speeds, but if it is possible, it will make use of routable ICMP requests for discovering the remote hosts on layer 3. If you use Wireshark to monitor the traffic, you will also see this, while a ping scan with nmap will be performed against all the hosts contained on a local network.

That is how easy the nmap tool is for you to use. It works by sending the ARP requests to a broadcast address for a series of IP addresses and it then it identifies the IP addresses by flagging of the responses. However, since the functionality has been integrated into nmap, you can execute it simply by giving it the right arguments.

Chapter 8- Banner Grabbing

Nmap comes with the Nmap Scripting Engine (NSE) which one can use so as to read banners from the network services which are running in the remote ports. In this chapter, we will demonstrate how to use the NSE so as to read the services so as to know the services which are associated with the open ports on the target system.

For you to be able to use the NSE for capturing the banners, you must have a remote system which is running network services which will disclose information once a network client has connected to them. You can use a Metasploit2 instance so as to do this.

The nmap NSE scripts can be called by use of the –script flag in the Nmap and then we specify the name of the script which is desired. For this script, we will use the –sT full-connect scan since the service banners can only be collected once a full TCP connection has been established. The script will have to be applied to the same ports scanned by a nmap request. This is shown below:

root@KaliLinux:~# nmap -sT 172.16.36.133 -p 22 --script=banner

Starting Nmap 6.25 (http://nmap.org) at 2017-7-27 04:56 EST

Nmap scan report for 172.16.36.133
Host is up (0.00036s latency).
PORT   STATE SERVICE
22/tcp open ssh
|_banner: SSH-2.0-OpenSSH_4.7p1 Debian-8ubuntu1
MAC Address: 00:0C:29:3D:84:32 (VMware)

Nmap done: 1 IP address (1 host up) scanned in 0.07 seconds

In this example, the TCP port 22 of a Metasploit2 system has been scanned. Rather than showing that the port is open, the nmap has used the banner script for collecting the service banner which is associated with the port. This technique can also be applied to the sequential range of ports by use of the – notation. This is shown below:

root@KaliLinux:~# nmap -sT 172.16.36.133 -p 1-100 --script=banner

Starting Nmap 6.25 (http://nmap.org) at 2013-12-19 04:56 EST

Nmap scan report for 172.16.36.133
Host is up (0.0024s latency).
Not shown: 94 closed ports
PORT   STATE SERVICE
21/tcp open ftp
|_banner: 220 (vsFTPd 2.3.4)
22/tcp open ssh
|_banner: SSH-2.0-OpenSSH_4.7p1 Debian-8ubuntu1
23/tcp open telnet
|_banner: \xFF\xFD\x18\xFF\xFD \xFF\xFD#\xFF\xFD'
25/tcp open smtp

|_banner: 220 metasploitable.localdomain ESMTP Postfix (Ubuntu)

53/tcp open domain
80/tcp open http
MAC Address: 00:0C:29:3D:84:32 (VMware)

Nmap done: 1 IP address (1 host up) scanned in 10.26 seconds

The NMAP SE script can also help us to perform a banner grabbing.

Chapter 9- Information Gathering

Nmap can be used for a number of activities in penetration testing. The Nmap Scripting Engine (NSE) helps in transforming the nmap into a multipurpose tool. It provides us with scripts which can help you in the stage for gathering information in a penetration test.

Our first step should be to determine the source of the IP address which is given to us by the client. There are a number of nmap scripts which can help us in this. The following command can help us to run all of these scripts:

Nmap - - script ip-geolocation-* hostname

In the above case, the hostname should be replaced by the name of the host, such as google.com etc. The script will call an external website so as to determine the coordinates and the location of the target.

We can also run the "shois" directly on the Linux terminal. You should note that nmap has a script which helps us use this script. The script will perform the same job that the command performs on a Linux system. When the script is executed, it will in turn give the registrar and the contact names. The following command demonstrates this:

nmap - - script whois hostname

When it comes to network penetration testing, email accounts are important, as they may provide information which may be used to accomplish the tests. For instance, the email names may be used as the username in social engineering engagements, that is, phishing attacks or if there is a need for one to carry out a brute force attack on a company's mail server. Nmap provides the following scripts which can be used for this job:

- http-google-email

- http-email-harvest

The first script, that is, http-google-email makes use of Google Groups and Google Web so as to search for the emails about the host in target. The second script, that is, http-email-harvest has to spider the web server so as to extract any email addresses which it discovers. The http-email-harvest script can be downloaded from the official website for nmap.

DNS records can also provide us with useful information during a penetration test. There are a number of tools which can help us to brute force DNS records, and these can give us better results. However, nmap also provides us with a script which can help us accomplish the same tasks, especially if we need to get DNS information during the nmap scans. The following command demonstrates how this can be done:

nmap –p80 - -script dns-brute hostname

That is how you can brute force DNS with nmap.

It is also possible for us to discover the additional hostnames which are based on a similar IP address with the http-reverse-ip nmap script. The script can help one to find the other web applications which exist on a similar web server. First download the script from the official nmap website.

The following command demonstrates how this script can be used:

nmap –p80 - -script http-reverse-ip hostname

Chapter 10- Penetrating into Servers

With the nmap tool, we are able to penetrate into a server, provided we know the port the server runs on. With nmap itself, we are able to perform a full penetration into a SQL database without the need for any other tool. In this chapter, we will show you how to penetrate into an SQL server and run some system commands through nmap.

In most cases, SQL databases run on port 1433, meaning that for you to be able to gather information about it, you have to first run the following command:

nmap –p1433 - -script ms-sql-info 192.168.1.77

This will give you all the SQL information which you need so as to penetrate into the SQL database. You will know the SQL version being used as well as the name of the name of the instance being used. Now that we have the above information, we can proceed to our next step. We should now check whether there is a weak password for authentication with the database. We will do this by use of an nmap script which will help us perform a brute force attack. The following command will help us achieve this:

nmap –p1433 - -script ms-sql-brute 192.168.1.77

If there are weak accounts in the system, they will be discovered. However, there may be none, and the above command may fail to discover any. In such a case, you will have to try your own usernames and passwords so as to carry out the brute force. The following command will help you achieve this:

nmap -p1433 –script ms-sql-brute –script-args userdb=/var/usernames.txt,passdb=/var/passwords.txt

Note that in the above command, we have passed in the files with the usernames and the ones with the passwords as arguments.

However, there is another script which can be used to check for null passwords on the Microsoft SQL Servers. The following script can help us achieve this:

nmap –p1433 - -script ms-sql-empty-password 192.168.1.77

The command will check for the null passwords in the SA accounts. Note that SA is a user in the SQL server.

In my case, I have noticed that the SA user has no password. Such information is useful, and it can be used to establish a connection with the database or run some other scripts which require us to have some valid user credentials. It is also possible for us to know the databases which the SA user is able to access or any other accounts which have been discovered. This is possible by running the ms-sql-hasdbaccess script together with the arguments given below:

nmap –p1433 - -script ms-sql-hasdbaccess.nse - -script –args mssql.username=sa 192.168.1.77

The SQL Server can also be queried through nmap so as to get the list of tables which we have. Here is the command for doing so:

nmap –p1433 - -script ms-sql-tables - -script –args mssql.username=sa 192.168.1.77

All the tables will be printed with details regarding their columns, their types, and their length.

If you are using the SQL Server 2000, the xp_cmdshell comes enabled by default, meaning that it is possible for you to run the operating system commands by use of the nmap scripts.

nmap –p1433 - -script ms-sql-dump-hashes - -script –args mssql.username=sa 192.168.1.77

Again, it is possible for you to run a script which will help you extract the hashed passwords from the database. You may ask yourself what such passwords may be used for. You can crack such passwords by use of tools like john the ripper. The following command will help you extract the hashed passwords from the database:

nmap –p1433 - -script ms-sql-xp-cmdshell - -script –args mssql.username=sa 192.168.1.77

If you have many accounts, then you will see the hashed passwords. In my case, I only have the SA account with a null password, so I don't get any result.

Conclusion

We have come to the end of this guide. Nmap stands for network mapper, and it is a tool which can be used for network scanning. The tool can help you to scan a network firewall and determine the ports which are open. With such information, one can take advantage of the open ports and penetrate into the firewall. With nmap, one can also determine the structure of the network behind the firewall. With such information, one can do a lot on the network. Nmap also allows one to determine the IP addresses of the network hosts. It is a good tool for penetration testers and hackers as it will help them gather network information and exploit some of the loopholes in their network. These can then be sealed before a malicious attacker can penetrate into the network.

Printed in Dunstable, United Kingdom